The ties that bind...

The ties that bind...

Life's
most
essential
knots
and ties

Stewart, Tabori & Chang · New York

Text copyright © 2004 Adrienne Ingrum, LLC
Illustrations copyright © 2004 Harry Bates

Designed by Larissa Nowicki
Edited by Marisa Bulzone
Graphic Production by Kim Tyner

Published in 2004 by
Stewart, Tabori & Chang
115 West 18th Street
New York, NY 10011

Canadian Distribution:
Canadian Manda Group
One Atlantic Avenue, Suite 105
Toronto, Ontario M6K 3E7
Canada

Library of Congress Cataloging-in-Publication Data

Oliver, Susan, 1972-
        The ties that bind / Susan Oliver ; illustrations by Harry Bates.–1st ed.
           p. cm.–(Finishing touches series)
        ISBN 1-58479-382-1
        1. Ribbon work. 2. Bows (Ribbon work) 3. Ropework. 4. Knots and splices.
        5. Scarves. 6. Neckties. I. Title. II. Series.

TT850.5.043 2004
745.5–dc22

                                                              2004004381

Printed in China by C&C Offset Ltd.

10 9 8 7 6 5 4 3 2 1

First Printing

Stewart, Tabori & Chang is a subsidiary of LA MARTINIÈRE

I would like to dedicate this book to my mother, Sue Oliver, who first inspired me toward creative pursuits. And to my family—my dad, Bob, Brenda and Bobby—I offer heartfelt thanks for their never-ending love, support, and belief.

I would like to thank Adrienne Ingrum for her faith in my ability, her helpful advice and her vision for this book. Her uplifting spirit and generous encouragement throughout the writing of this book made the entire process enjoyable. My gratitude to Marisa Bulzone for her valuable suggestions and for being such a wonderful editor to work with; Trudi Bartow for her tireless research and assistance; Larissa Nowicki for the elegant design; and Ana Deboo for her thoughtful and excellent copyediting. A special thanks to Toni Barton for her tireless effort, skill, and patience in working with me to photograph the steps. Without their able contribution, this book would not have been possible.

Introduction

Ties, which though light as air,
are as strong as links of iron.

EDMUND BURKE

**"Voilà!" the attendant behind the counter says as she
hands you a beautifully wrapped gift.** Eyeing the artful bow,
you wonder if you too can produce the same lovely result. You have
a black-tie engagement to attend, and you cannot remember the last
time you tied a formal bow. There is a pile of wood in your backyard
that you'd like to transport and have no idea how to bundle the logs
securely. You have purchased a scarf because you love the color
or print and now wonder how to transform that beautiful square or
rectangular piece of cloth into a decorative accent. The skill of
tying can make all the difference. **The ties that bind...** will clearly
demonstrate a variety of techniques for creating bows, knots, and
decorative ties.

Like the other books in the **Finishing Touches** series, **The ties
that bind...** celebrates handcrafts, which are making a revival as
growing numbers of people seek simpler, more satisfying ways to
live. It is rewarding to sit back and look at a wrapped gift, complete
with exquisite bow, and know that you created it. It is gratifying when
you can enhance your classic black suit with a cleverly tied scarf.
And it is absolutely pleasing to enjoy the draping fronds of your
favorite potted fern as it hangs elegantly from the ceiling, knowing
that you accomplished the task with the simple technique of tying a

cat's paw knot. ***The ties that bind...*** highlights the emotional benefit that comes with using one's hands to make ordinary objects more beautiful and individual.

Bows, knots, and decorative ties are a quick way to add an element of self-expression to clothing, the home, and, of course, wrappings. Decorative knots can inexpensively add beauty to the functional and the frivolous. Using clear language and illustrations, the projects in this book guide you through each step, from selecting necessary materials to putting on the finishing touches.

What to Keep on Hand

A jewel which she takes
From off her head, and that she makes
Ulysses on his bosom wear,
About his neck, she ties it there.

HOMER, *THE ODYSSEY*

Learning the technique of tying will open the door to your creative knot-making world. But before you begin there are a few basic supplies you will need to keep on hand. With the suggested materials in your arsenal you will never be caught off guard or in want of any supply needed to tie the perfect knot. Making sure what you need is on hand will save time, as well as take a load off your mind. You will already have the ribbon you need to make a beautiful bow, the string you need to bundle a package, and the appropriate tool to cut your materials with. You will be ready to make the practical or decorative knot you desire.

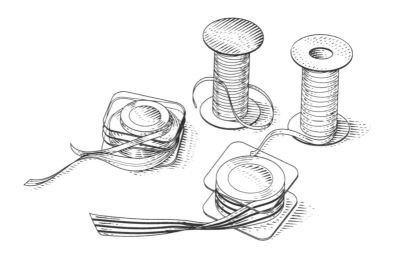

Ribbon

Ribbon comes in a variety of colors, materials (satin, velvet, cotton, silk, organza, wired ribbon, grosgrain, moiré, and many more), and widths ($\frac{1}{8}$ inch to 5 inches). Each style creates a different feeling. Keeping a good variety on hand ensures that you will be able to put the perfect finishing touches on any gift you wrap. A basic collection might include satin, chiffon, organza, and velvet ribbons in red, blue, pink, white, silver, and gold.

Sharp Scissors

There are many different types of scissors available. Some features to consider when purchasing scissors are the weight, size, type of blade, comfort of finger holes, and material you intend to cut. Eight-inch forged-steel (high-carbon, cast steel) dressmaker shears with bent handles will provide good weight and the sharp, clean edge needed for cutting most medium–to-heavyweight fabrics and ribbons. Scissors with micro-serrated edges can be used for cutting silk, rayon, and other delicate fabrics and ribbons. Lightweight 8-inch all-purpose scissors with stainless-steel blades are best for cutting paper. It is important to remember that individual scissors should be used solely for one purpose. The same scissors that are used to cut fabric should not be used to cut paper or any other material. This will allow you to make clean cuts as well as preserve the sharpness and life span of the scissors.

Test scissors prior to purchase by opening and closing them several times. Good-quality scissors should operate smoothly and easily. Craft, notion, and sewing stores will carry a variety of scissors.

Florist Wire

Florist wire is a thin, flexible wire that is either painted or wrapped with cloth tape. It is easily bent with the hands and often used in creating floral arrangements. It comes in a variety of colors (green, white, brown, silver, and gold), varying gauge sizes, and is sold in precut stems or wrapped around paddles or spools. A thin gauge such as 24 or 26 is ideal for securing any type of bow. (The larger the gauge number, the thinner the wire.) You can find florist wire in any floral or craft store.

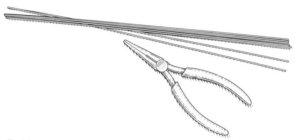

Wire Cutter

A garden or florist pruner is an ideal multipurpose tool that can be used for cutting florist wire. When purchasing a pruner, look for a 7-inch tool with a straight steel blade and a notched counter blade. Alternatively, a 6-inch wire cutter with a steel blade can be used for cutting florist wire. Whichever tool you choose, look for one with a nonstick rubberized handle. Cutters can be found at hardware or craft stores.

Rope, Twine, and String

Rope consists of multiple strands of twisted or braided fiber, which can be natural or man-made, and is $1/8$ inch or larger in diameter. It is suitable for tying, hanging, and anchoring heavy bundles or objects. Polypropylene rope is lightweight, chemical-resistant, and resists abrasion. It has a high melting point, excellent shock absorption, and will stretch about 25 percent before breaking. It is economical and stores well in wet and dry environments. Manila hemp rope is a low-stretch rope that holds knots well. It does not melt, has average abrasion resistance, poor chemical resistance, and must be stored in a dry location. Keep your project in mind when choosing the type of rope that will best suit your needs. Hemp rope is a good choice for bundling or binding, while polypropylene rope will provide the strength and support you will need if your project involves hanging, anchoring, or pulling.

Twine consists of twisted strands of man-made or natural fiber less than 5mm in diameter. It comes in a variety of colors and sizes (1.5mm to 5mm). Nylon and hemp twine are strong and durable. Hemp twine has the benefit of being biodegradable, while nylon twine is preferable for its endurance. Both are perfect for tying packages, tall vines, and garden plants and can also be used in jewelry making, beading, candle wicking, and macramé.

Cotton string is a lightweight, all-purpose tool for tying packages and bags, binding lightweight objects around the house, and tying meats in cooking.

Rope, twine, and string come in handy when you least expect it. Perhaps you need to prepare a roast, bundle magazines and newspapers for recycling, or pull up a small tree that a sudden, unexpected storm has knocked down. Keeping a supply of three-strand twisted manila and polypropylene rope, nylon and hemp twine, and cotton string ensures that you will have the proper tool when the need arises. Look for rope, twine, and string at your local hardware, outdoor sporting goods, or craft store.

Rope Cutter

A sturdy box cutter, utility knife, or knife with a folding blade cuts rope, twine, and string easily and cleanly. Look for a tool with a comfortable grip that won't slip in your hands. Handles made of synthetic plastics and fiberglass are lightweight and allow for a firm, controlled grip in all weather. A rope knife can be purchased at any hardware or outdoor sporting goods store.

Yardstick

There are several tools that measure length—yardstick, ruler, carpenter's tape measure, and seamstress' measuring tape—but the yardstick is best suited to the projects in this book. Whether made of wood or plastic, it is a useful tool for measuring out lengths of rope, ribbon, paper, and fabric because of its length and rigidity. Choose a yardstick with clear, readable markings. You can purchase this tool at a fabric or notion store.

Storing Your Materials

Loosely bound
By countless silken ties of love and thought
To everything on earth the compass round.

ROBERT FROST, *THE SILKEN TENT*

Have you ever thrown out a ball of string because you could not unravel it? Have you ever searched endlessly through a container of tangled ribbon looking for the color you need? Have you ever wondered how to handle those yards of excess rope? Now that you've invested in the supplies you need for tying, how do you keep them neat and easily accessible? This next section offers ways to store your materials. Proper storage will not only keep your life hassle free, but also extend the life of your materials.

Ribbon

To keep ribbons orderly and easy to find, store them by color in a lidded container or box. A few simple precautions will keep you from ending up with a tangled mess. Begin by taping down the free end of the ribbon roll with masking tape, then place the roll in a small clear plastic bag. Organize the bags vertically side by side in the box. If your ribbon is not on a roll, cut a section from a paper towel roll that is slightly larger than the width of your ribbon and tape one end of the ribbon to the cardboard. Wrap the ribbon around the roll and tape the free end down.

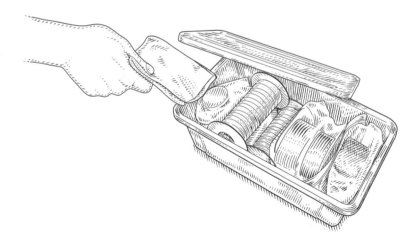

Rope

Store rope neatly by tying it using the buntline or gasket coil knot (see page 35–36), and it will remain tangle-free. Keep the rope dry by storing it in a box with a tight lid.

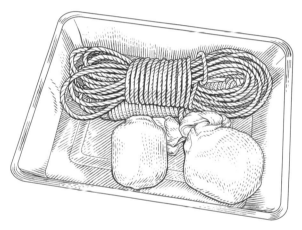

Twine/String

Twine and string are usually sold in balls, and keeping them from unraveling can be a headache. Here you can put to use the sock that has lost its mate or the pantyhose that have a run. Stuffing the ball into a sock or pantyhose will keep it from unraveling and becoming a tangled mess. Keep the socks/pantyhose in a storage or filing container with a tight lid to prevent moisture from entering.

Cutting Tools

Store cutting tools flat to keep the points sharp. Place them in a cool, dry place to prevent the steel from rusting.

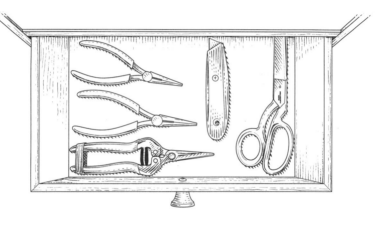

➤ *Cutting Tool Maintenance* *When investing in good-quality cutting tools, preserve their sharpness and extend their lives by having them professionally sharpened twice a year. (Sharpening is not recommended for serrated blades.) Wipe the blades with a clean, dry cloth after every use to prevent them from rusting.*

Knots You Should Know

> Man is a knot, a web, a mesh into which
> relationships are tied.
>
> ANTOINE DE SAINT-EXUPÉRY, *FLIGHT TO ARRAS*

Knot tying is perhaps one of the oldest techniques in existence. Knots have been discovered at sites of ancient civilizations where they were used as means of record keeping and communication. For centuries, fishermen and sailors have been experts in the art of knot making. There can be no doubt that knowing how to tie a secure knot is a valuable skill.

The knot itself is a versatile tool. Knots can be used around the home, outdoors, for rescue. Knots range from simple to complex and can be fashioned with varying levels of strength, tension, and security. There are binding knots, securing knots, hanging knots, and decorative knots. Each has its own benefit. Knowing the right knot to use at the opportune moment can get one out of a bind!

Square Knot

The square knot is the most basic and useful of knots. It can be used to tie any item quickly and easily and has the added benefit of strength. Many of the ties and knots described throughout this book will call for this knot.

1. Hold the ends of the cord to be tied between the thumb and forefinger of each hand. Cross the left end over the right end.

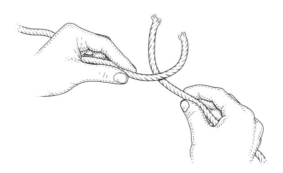

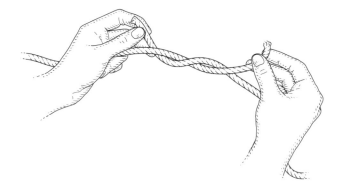

2. Pull the bottom end over then under the loop, making sure to keep the tie taut.
3. Cross the right end over the left end.
4. Ring the bottom end over and through the new loop that is formed.
5. Pull the ends tight.

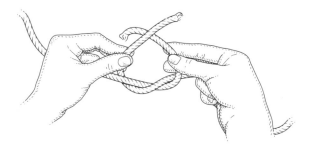

Cat's Paw

This knot, often used in fishing to attach a line to a hook, is also ideal for hanging objects such as a planter or fruit basket because it provides strong support by evenly distributing weight over two loops.

1. Hold the rope between the thumb and forefinger of each hand, ensuring that there is about 20 inches of slack between the hands.

2. Twist the rope away from you three or more full turns with both hands. There will be a loop where your thumb and forefinger hold the rope on each end.

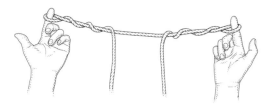

3. Bring the two loops together.

4. Pull down on the tail of the rope.

5. Place the loops over the hook.

6. Using a square knot (page 22–23) or a surgeon's knot (page 30–31), the tails of the rope can be attached to the sides of the object to be hung.

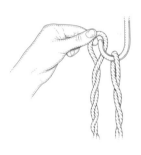

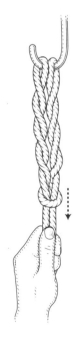

Slipknot

Often used in knitting as the first "cast on" stitch, this knot can be employed when a simple but secure attachment is required. The loop of this knot can be slipped onto any object and pulled tight.

1. Form a loop by crossing the left end of the rope over the right end, holding tight where the ropes intersect.
2. Wrap the topmost end of the rope underneath and through the loop to form a second loop.
3. Pull on the opposite end to tighten the slipknot.

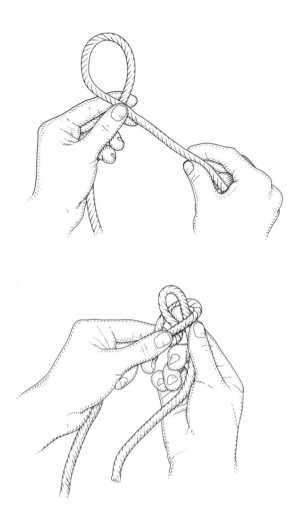

Duffel Bag or Pouch Knot

This knot uses the slipknot (page 26–27) to quickly secure
a small pouch or name tag to a duffel bag or suitcase.

1. Attach the cord to the pouch or tag by placing one end of the
   cord through the hole or opening in the tag. Form a double
   cord by bringing the two free ends of the cord together and
   tying a knot.

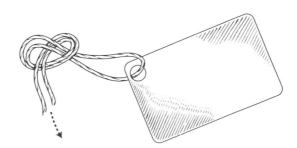

2. Hold the double cord with the knotted end in the left hand. Cross the left end of the cord over the right end and pull through the loop to form a second loop.

3. Pull on the end attached to the tag to tighten the slipknot.

4. Using this knot with a tag, you can now attach it to any object with a handle by wrapping the loop around the handle and pulling the tag through the loop.

5. Pull tight to secure the tag.

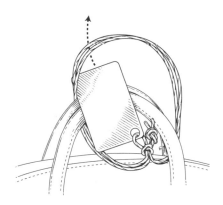

Surgeon's Knot

The surgeon's knot derives its name from its use in medicine. Surgeons use this knot to tie off sutures because it provides a strong, secure hold that is not easily undone. For practical use it is usually tied with twine.

1. Begin by holding one end of the twine in each hand. Cross the left end over and under the right end, pulling through the loop.
2. Wrap the same end (now at the right) over and under the right side of the loop again, pulling it through a second time.
3. Cross the twine held in your right hand over and under the left end, pulling through the second loop.
4. Pull tight to secure.

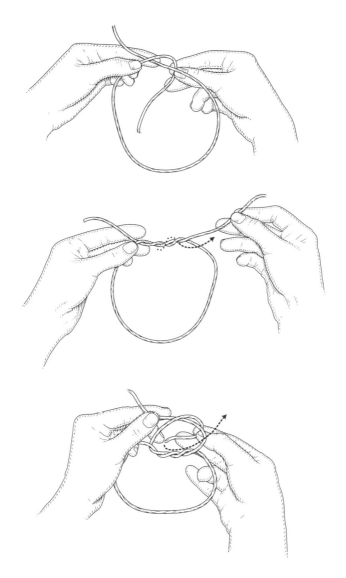

Packer's Knot

This knot is useful in the kitchen to bind roasts and legs but can also be used for tying parcels or bundles.

1. Begin by placing the object horizontally before you. Wrap the twine around the object, leaving a tail of approximately 8 inches on the top end of the cord. Depending on the thickness of your twine, you may require more than 8 inches for the tail.

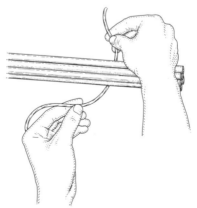

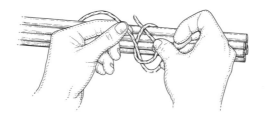

2. Wrap the top cord around the bottom cord, crossing it back under itself to form a loop.
3. Bring the end of the cord over the top cord and through the loop from right to left. Pull tight.

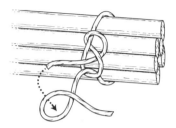

4. Form a loop with the bottom cord by crossing it over itself.

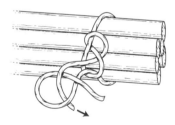

5. Place the top end of the cord through the loop in the bottom cord.

6. Pull tight to secure the knot.

Buntline or Gasket Coil

This tie is helpful in securing rope for storage or gathering up excess rope to keep it out of the way.

1. Begin by coiling the rope: Bend your arm at the elbow, then form an L shape with your forefinger and thumb. Hold one end of the rope between the L shape and continuously wrap the rope around your elbow and through the L shape until it is almost completely coiled. Leave a tail of about 1-inch for every foot of rope that is being coiled. The length of the tail will vary with thickness of the rope. Thinner rope requires a shorter tail while thicker rope requires a longer tail.

2. Grasp the coiled rope securely at its center. Wrap the tail horizontally around the coiled rope four or five times.

3.   Form a loop by pulling the tail end of the rope partially through the center of the coil above the wrapping.

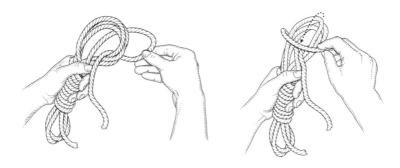

4.   Bring this loop down over the coil around the front.
5.   Pull the tail to secure the wrapping.

Untying and Untangling

Your patience is at an end! You've tossed that tangled mass of rope into the dark recesses of your garage or storage room. Or perhaps you've given up your endless struggle to untie that stubborn knot. Well, untying a knot or untangling rope might seem a daunting, near-impossible task, but with a few tricks the impossible can be achieved with miraculous ease.

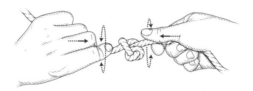

Untying a Jammed Knot

1. Grasp the rope near the knot, holding one end in each hand.
2. Moving your hands in opposite directions, quickly and firmly twist the rope back and forth while pushing toward the knot.
3. Continue in the above manner. The pressure will loosen the knot so that you are able to untie it.

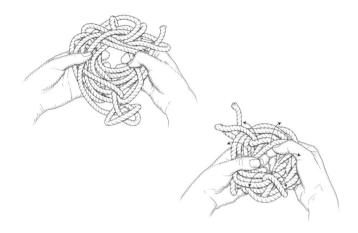

Untangling Rope

1. Loosen all knots and jams in the rope and open a hole in the tangle where the longest end of the rope leaves the snarl.

2. Grip each hand around the sides of the tangled rope so that your fingers rise up through the hole in the center of the tangle. Using a rolling motion, move your fists under and through the open hole.

3. Continue to "roll" in this manner until you are able to free the end of the rope from the snarl. Do not pull on the end, but rather allow it to release itself with your gentle rolling motion. Keep the snarl open and loose.

4. Continue until the rope is untangled. With patience, any snarl can be resolved this way.

Beautifully Wrapped

True love's the gift which God has given . . .
The silver link, the silken tie,
Which heart to heart and mind to mind
In body and in soul can bind.
SIR WALTER SCOTT, *LAY OF THE LAST MINSTREL*

An exquisitely tied bow can add elegance to the simplest of wrappings. Whether you choose a ribbon of velvet or satin, felt or burlap, lace or chiffon, with even the most basic bow a brown-paper package suddenly becomes a beautiful gift; a plain parcel is transformed into a present worthy of kings and queens. And the gift becomes a representation of the giver's heart.

A bow of convoluted twists and folds appears complicated, but tying one need not be.

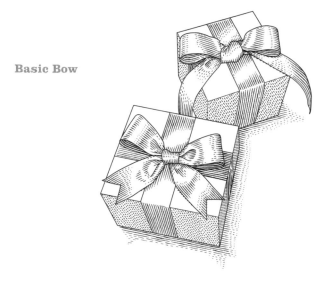

Basic Bow

1. To estimate the amount of ribbon needed, loosely wrap the ribbon around the length and width of the box. Allow an extra 24 inches of ribbon on each end for the bow.

2. Place the ribbon vertically across the top of the box, then wrap the ribbon around the length and hold it at the bottom of the box.

3. Beneath the box, making sure that the wrong side of the ribbon is flat against the box, twist the ribbons around each other 90 degrees so that each end of the ribbon is pulled horizontally. Adjust the ribbon, if necessary, by twisting or turning the ends to ensure that the wrong side remains flat against the box. Bring the ends back up and around the center width of the box. Pull firmly to keep the ribbon taut.

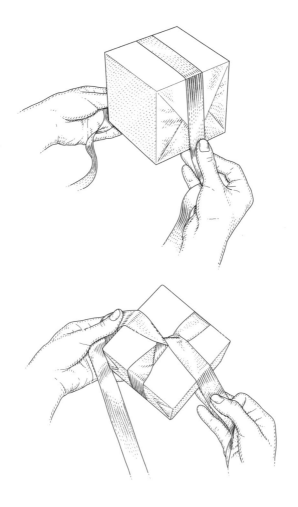

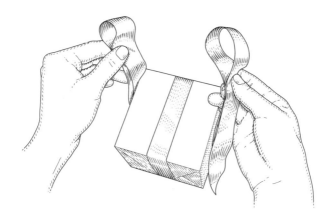

4. Fold both ends of the ribbon into two equal loops of about 4 $\frac{1}{2}$ inches.

5. Cross the right loop over the left, then fold it beneath the left loop, bringing it toward you. Pull firmly.

6. Cross the left loop over the right loop. Place the left loop though the hole beneath the right loop to create the knot. Pull taut and trim the ribbon ends to the desired length.

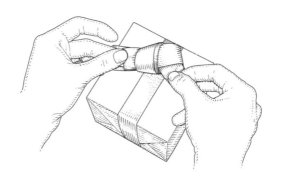

Floral Bow

1. Cut a piece of ribbon 45 inches long or longer. Make a 1-inch loop about 8 inches from the ribbon end. Pinch the ribbon between your thumb and forefinger to hold the loop securely.

2. With the long end of the ribbon, make a 1-inch loop to the left of the pinched loop.

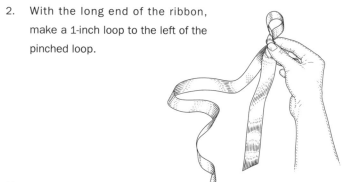

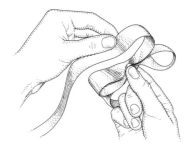

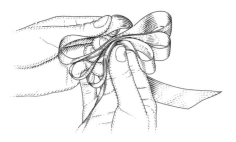

3. Continue to make loops, alternating from right to left and gradually increasing the size of the loops for each pair. Keep the ribbon securely pinched between your thumb and forefinger. Make three or more loops on each side.

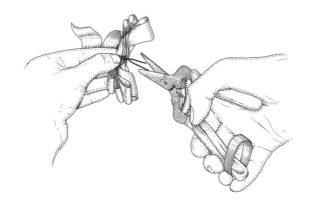

4. Wrap a 3-inch piece of florist wire around the center of the bow. Twist the wire tightly to secure the bow. Trim excess wire.

5. Fan out the loops so that they resemble the petals of a flower.

6. Trim the tails of the ribbon to the same length, cutting ends at an angle.

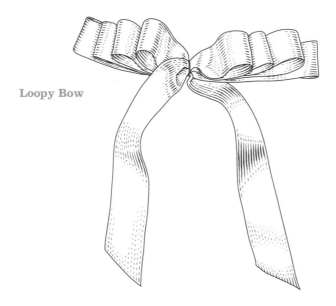

Loopy Bow

1. Cut a piece of ribbon approximately 60 inches long. Leaving a tail of about 8 inches, make a 3-inch loop toward the left.

2. Holding the ribbon between the thumb and forefinger, make a loop toward the right the same length as the left loop.

3. Continue making loops that are the same size, alternating from left to right. Make four or more loops on each side of the pinch.

4. Secure the bow by wrapping a 3-inch piece of florist wire around the center of the loops. Twist the wire at the back of the bow and cut away excess wire.

5. Fluff out the loops and trim the tails of the ribbon to the same length by cutting the ends at an angle.

Scarves as Instant Accents

I am always tying up
and then deciding to depart.
FRANK O'HARA, *TO THE HARBORMASTER*

A scarf is a great way to add color to or change the look and style of your current wardrobe. With infinite prints and colors available, scarves can be your tools to create limitless style options. Your favorite scarf can be either casual or elegant depending on what you wear it with. The "head wrap" with jeans and a white shirt is perfect for a day at the shore. The "head wrap" with a simple black dress will turn heads on your way to work. With imagination, the possibilities are endless.

Head Wrap

1. Begin with a scarf 3 feet square. Fold the scarf diagonally, forming a triangle.

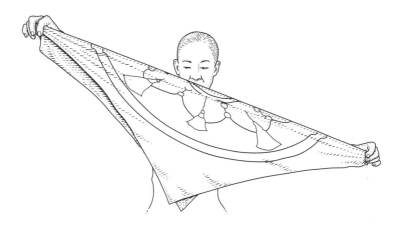

2. Place the scarf around the head with the folded edge facing forward.

3. Wrap the left and right pointed ends of the scarf around the front of the neck. Using a square knot (page 22–23), tie the ends at the back of the neck.

Long Tie

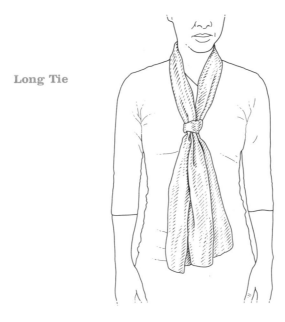

1. Using an oblong scarf about 11 inches by 58 inches, make a band by folding it in half lengthwise. If necessary, fold the scarf lengthwise a second time so that the width is about 5 inches.

2. Place the folded scarf around the neck. Form a loop halfway down the left end of the scarf and make a loose knot by pulling the left end of the scarf through the loop.

3. Bring the right end of the scarf through the center of the knot and adjust the ends until they are even.

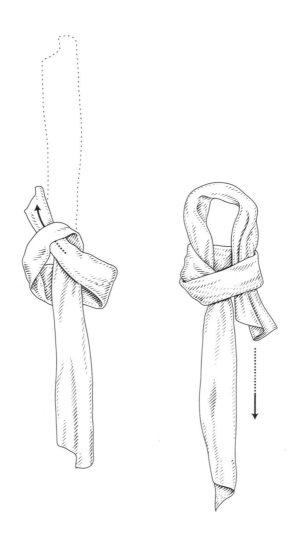

Neck Wrap

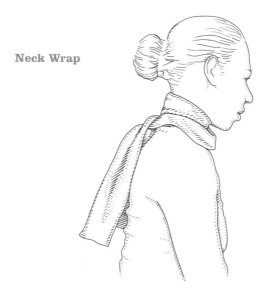

1. Using an oblong scarf about 11 inches by 58 inches, make a band by folding it in half lengthwise. If necessary, fold the scarf lengthwise a second time so that the width is about 5 inches.
2. Place the folded scarf around the neck. At the base of the neck, twist the ends of the scarf around each other twice.
3. Wrap the ends of the scarf behind the neck and, using a square knot (page 22–23), tie them securely.

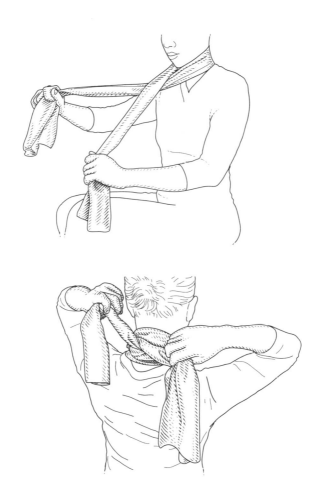

Two-Shoulder Wrap

1. Begin with a scarf about 33 inches square. Fold the scarf in half diagonally, forming a triangle.

2. Place the scarf about the shoulders with the folded edge on top.

3. Using a square knot (page 22–23), tie the ends in front.

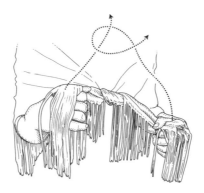

Side-Knotted Belt

1. Begin with an oblong scarf about
    11 inches by 58 inches. Fold it in
    half lengthwise twice.

2. Wrap the scarf around the hips and tie it on the side, using a
    square knot (page 22–23).
3. Spread out the folds of the part of the scarf that surrounds
    your hips.

Graceful Sarongs

The way to rear up children (to be just),
They know a simple, merry, tender knack
Of tying sashes, fitting baby-shoes,
And stringing pretty words that make no sense,
And kissing full sense into empty words.

ELIZABETH BARRETT BROWNING, *AURORA LEIGH*

The sarong, or pareo, is a versatile and beautiful wardrobe treasure.
The traditional clothing of Indonesian women, the sarong can be
functional as well as decorative, both casual and elegant. Made
from silk or cotton or rayon, it can be intricately dyed, embroidered,
or plain. There is no limit to what a sarong can be.

The average dimension of a sarong is 68 inches by 44 inches.
Its very size allows for diversity of use. Following are some ideas on
how to fashion a sarong into a wearable style, but keep in mind that
it can also dress up your home as a tablecloth, wall hanging,
or lightweight blanket.

Classic Skirt

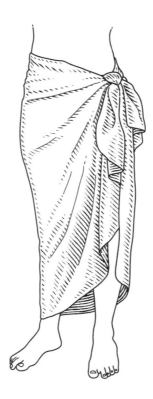

1. Begin by holding the sarong horizontally.

2. Wrap the sarong around the hips once or twice.

3. Using a square knot (page 22–23), secure the ends in front or on the side.

4. A shorter skirt can be made by first folding the sarong in half horizontally, then following the above steps.

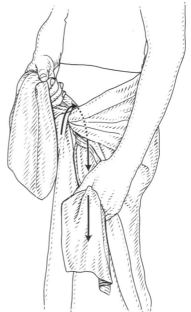

Classic Dress

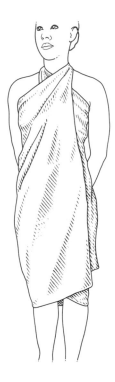

1. Begin by holding the sarong horizontally.
2. Wrap the sarong around your back,
   holding the corners out in front.

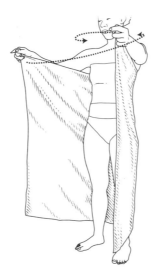

3. Twist each end of the sarong once, then wrap the ends around your neck and tie them in back using a square knot (page 22–23).

4. As a variation, eliminate the twist before wrapping the ends around the neck.

Rio Dress

1. Begin by holding the sarong horizontally.
2. Wrap the sarong around your back, holding the corners out in front. Tie the ends into a small square knot (page 22–23).
3. Loop the knotted ends around your neck.

4. Pull down the side edges in front.

5. Using your thumbs, grab the edges of the sarong under each arm and pull out.

6. Wrap the edges under the breasts and fasten the ends using a square knot or pin.

Strap Dress

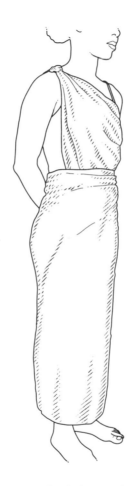

1. This dress is meant to be tied over a bathing suit. Begin by holding the sarong horizontally.

2. Wrap the sarong around your back, holding the corners out in front. Cross one end over the front of your body and pull it beneath the shoulder strap of your bathing suit.

3. Form a loop by pulling the end of sarong beneath your bathing suit strap a second time, then pull the end of the sarong through the loop to form a knot.
4. Wrap the other end of the sarong around your waist, tucking it in at your side.

Tie A Tie

I don't want them to come in with a white tie,
And I don't want them to come in a black tie.
But I do want them to come in a tie.

RUDOLF BING

The necktie, or cravat, has an ancient history that can be traced back to the Roman Empire, where men wrapped cloth around their necks to keep their throats warm. These neck cloths were more functional but the practice has since developed into a fashionable means of expression. In less ancient times, neckties were also used to distinguish and exclude. Often the manner in which the necktie was knotted indicated membership in a certain organization or club. The basic "Four-in-Hand" knot prevalent today is one example—the Four-in-Hand was a nineteenth-century gentleman's club in London. A tie well knotted was then, and can still be, the making of a man. Just as the cut of a suit—double-breasted, single-breasted, four-button, sports, tuxedo—is an expression of a man's character and individuality, a necktie, with its variety of fabrics, textures, and colors, is an added manifestation of his uniqueness, elegance, and style.

Formal Bow

The bow tie owes its roots to the cravat, a rectangular neck cloth worn by Croatian soldiers in the seventeenth century. Largely due to Louis XIV's admiration of these soldiers' cravats, what eventually became known as the bow tie gained a popularity that has withstood the test of time. Today the bow tie is the standard tie worn with formal eveningwear.

1. Place the tie around the neck so that the right end is $1\frac{1}{2}$ inches longer than the left.
2. Cross the right end over the left and bring it up and under the left.

3. Fold the other end of the tie into a horizontal loop, forming what will be the right bow. Drop the loose end over the loop.

4. Fold the loose end to make a similar bow.

5. Bring this partial loop through the hole formed beneath the right bow. Pull tight.

6. Placing an index finger in each bow and the thumb on the outside edge of the bow, gently adjust the shape of the tie so that both bows are even.

Pratt (Shelby) Knot

In the 1980s the Pratt knot became the first new knot to be identified by the Neckwear Association of America in fifty years. Mr. Jerry Pratt, a former employee at the United States Chamber of Commerce, created this knot. However, when Don Shelby, a popular television anchorman and radio show host in Minnesota, was seen wearing the Pratt knot on TV, he was given the credit as its inventor.

The Pratt knot is a semiwide knot and, uniquely, is begun with the tie wrong-side out.

1.   Begin with the underside of the tie facing out. The tip of the wide end should be about 8 to 10 inches lower than the narrow end. Place the wide end of the tie under the narrow end.

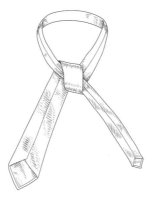

2.   Wrap the wide end over the narrow end, forming a loop. Place the wide end down through the neck loop. Pull down gently on the ends to tighten.

3.   Wrap the wide end over the narrow end again.

4.   Pull the wide end up behind the tie and through the neck loop.

5.   Pull the wide end down through the knot and gently tighten. The tip of the wide end should touch the belt buckle.

The Ascot

The ascot derives its name from England's Royal Ascot race where this form of tie was first worn. Since the race's inception the men's dress code at Royal Ascot has mandated formal attire, including neckwear. Today, the ascot is not only an option for those who attend the yearly race, but also a choice accompaniment to formal morning wear and wedding attire. The ascot can also be worn instead of a traditional necktie for casual engagements.

For formal dress, the ascot is worn with a wing-tip collar shirt and tied outside the shirt collar in the same manner as a conventional necktie. When dress is casual, the ascot can be worn inside an open shirt collar.

1. For casual dress, leave the neck of the shirt open. Place the ascot around the neck with the right end extending 6 inches below the left end. For formal dress, begin by placing the ascot around the buttoned shirt collar.

2. Wrap the right end over and underneath the left end.

3. Bring that same end over and under the other end a second time.

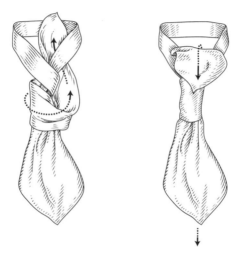

4. Pull the right end upward through the loop at the neck.
5. Allow the fabric to fall over the bottom end.
6. Adjust the ascot at the throat to cover the knot.
7. For casual dress, tuck the ends of the ascot inside your shirtfront. For formal dress, tuck the ends of the ascot inside your vest.

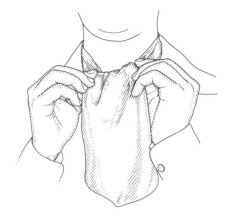

Neckwear Maintenance

- Give your ties two or three days rest between wearings to allow the wrinkles to smooth out.

- Always unknot your tie completely when taking it off. Never slip it over your head.

- Do not untie the knot by pulling on the small end. Always reverse the knot-tying process itself.

- Do not make your knots too tight.

Bibliography and Resources

*Poets don't draw. They unravel their handwriting
and then tie it up again, but differently.*

JEAN COCTEAU

The Complete Book of Knots
Geoffrey Budworth, The Lyons Press, New York, 1997

Handbook of Knots
Des Pawson, DK Publishing, New York, 1998

Creative Giftwraps
Constance Richards, Sterling Publishing, New York, 2001

50 Easy Ways to Tie a Scarf
Julie Claire, Pocket Books, New York, 1992

How to Tie a Tie
Michael Adam, Pocket Books, New York, 1992

Craft, Notion, and Specialty Stores

Fancy Ribbon www.fancyribbon.com

Jo-Ann Stores www.joann.com

Kate's Paperie www.katespaperie.com

Michaels Stores www.michaels.com

Paper Mart www.papermart.com

Saveoncrafts www.save-on-crafts.com

Hardware Stores

Home Depot www.homedepot.com

Lowes Home Improvement www.lowes.com

Restoration Hardware www.restorationhardware.com

Outdoor Sporting Goods Retailers

Eastern Mountain Sports www.ems.com

Oshman www.oshmans.com

Paragon www.paragonsports.com

REI www.rei.com

The Sports Authority www.thesportsauthority.com

Sharpening Services

Cutting-Solutions www.cutting-solutions.com

Elmer's Clipper Service www.elmersclipperservice.com

Platz's Sharpening www.platzenterprise.com

Susan Oliver's first love is the arts. She began drawing, painting, and writing in childhood, and not wanting to be limited to the classic arts, she learned to sew by watching her mother. As a young girl, she began designing clothes for her many dolls and her younger sister, as well as herself. Her interest in clothing led her to create costumes for dramatic, musical, and ballet productions. She currently designs and sews wedding gowns and couture dresses.

Susan earned her B.A. in English literature, fine arts, and psychology from Stanford University and her M.A. in art therapy from New York University.

She lives in Los Angeles.